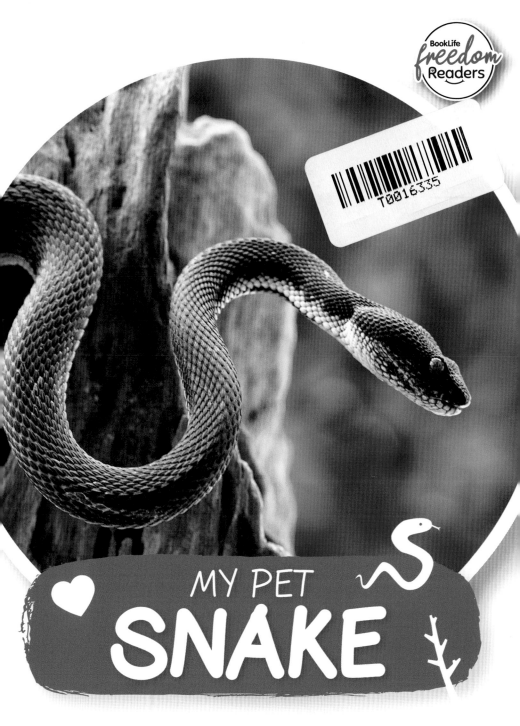

MY PET
SNAKE

BY WILLIAM ANTHONY

BookLife
PUBLISHING

©2022
BookLife Publishing Ltd.
King's Lynn
Norfolk PE30 4LS

A catalogue record for
this book is available from
the British Library.

ISBN: 978-1-80155-136-6

Written by:
William Anthony

Edited by:
Madeline Tyler

Designed by:
Jasmine Pointer

All facts, statistics, web addresses and URLs in this book were verified as valid and accurate at time of writing. No responsibility for any changes to external websites or references can be accepted by either the author or publisher.

Photocredits:
Images are courtesy of Shutterstock.com. With thanks to Getty Images, Thinkstock Photo and iStockphoto.

Front cover - Duplass, dangdumrong. 2 - Krisda Ponchaipulltawee. 3 - Eric Isselee, Kuznetsov Alexey. 4 - Duplass. 5 - Lana Langlois. 6 - BIGANDT.COM. 7 - VinceBradley. 8 - Sergey Novikov. 9 - halimqd. 10 - SasinTipchai. 11 - Duplass. 12 - Marek Velechovsky. 13 - Skynavin. 14 - Supershine. 15 - pattyphotoart. 16 - pixinoo. 17 - Eric Isselee. 18 - getideaka. 19 - Mark_Kostich. 20 - Tom Grundy. 21 - Somporn Pramong. 22 - Africa Studio. 23 - Sergey Novikov.

BookLife
freedom
Readers

CONTENTS

Jay ♥ and Monty

Hello! My name is Jay, and this is my pet snake, Monty.
He is twelve years old. Snakes are my favourite animal
because they have cool patterns on them.

Jay →

4

Whether you are thinking about getting one, or you have had one for a little while, Monty and I are going to take you through how to look after a snake.

Monty

Getting a Snake

Looking after a snake means you are going to have a lot of responsibility. You will need to feed them and give them a nice home with lots of places to hide.

My family got Monty from a pet shop, but you can get snakes from other places too. You can also get a snake from a breeder. This is someone who keeps snakes to mate them. Research the person or place you are buying a pet from to make sure they care for their animals properly.

Home

Snakes need a very special type of home. Your snake will need to be kept in a vivarium. A vivarium is like a house for your snake, but it has glass walls. The glass stops your snake from escaping.

A vivarium also keeps things nice and warm for your snake. Snakes are cold blooded, so your vivarium will need to be warm at one end and cool at the other.

Viper snake in the wild

Playtime

Different types of snakes like doing different things. Leave lots of branches and rocks in their vivarium so they have things to climb.

Monty likes coming out to play with us. All snakes are different, so do not force your snake to play with you if they do not want to. Always be calm and gentle with your snake. My dad and my sister are good at playing with Monty.

Food

Feeding time is the least fun part of looking after a snake. Snakes usually eat dead mice or rats. Your snake will need to be fed once a week.

When your snake knows that food is coming, they can get very excited. They might even think your hand is food by accident. It is a good idea to get an adult to feed your snake. Snakes can be dangerous pets.

Bedtime zZ

Snakes are not like us when they sleep. We sleep at night after a long day, but snakes can sleep at any time – this could be at night or during the day. Snakes do not have eyelids, so they still look awake when they are asleep!

You could put a little cave or a pile of bark in your snake's vivarium. This is a nice, dark place for your snake to take a little nap.

The Vet

Snakes can get ill, just like humans. Snakes that are ill can go to the vets. Vets are like doctors, but for animals instead of humans. They will do everything they can to help your snake get better again.

One day when I came home, Monty was breathing loudly from his mouth. Snakes should breathe from their nostrils. I told my parents, and we took him to the vets who made him better again. Make sure you tell someone if you think your snake is unwell.

Growing Up

It can be hard to tell when your snake is getting old. Sometimes old snakes will get a bit bonier, or they might need longer breaks between feeds.

As your snake grows up, you might notice them start to shed their skin. All animals lose old, dead skin, but must do so slowly. Snakes lose their old skin all in one go!

Super Snakes

All pet snakes are amazing, but some wild snakes are simply super. There is a type of snake in Asia with a very special trick...

... it can fly! The flying snake jumps from tree to tree by moving its body in an 'S' shape. Do not expect your snake to be able to fly, though – flying snakes have adapted to do this.

You 💙 and Your Pet

Whether you have got your snake or you are about to get one, make sure you take care of them just like Monty and I have taught you.

I am sure you will make a great pet owner. Try to think of what your snake would like in the wild and make their vivarium like that. Most of all, make sure you enjoy your new scaly friend.

QUESTIONS ??

1: What is a vivarium?

2: What should you put in a vivarium?

3: What do snakes usually eat?
a) Chocolate
b) Grass
c) Dead mice or rats

4: If your snake is ill, who can help it get better?

5: What would you call your pet snake?